THE
VOCAL SKILLS
POCKETBOOK

By Richard Payne
Drawings by Phil Hailstone

"Everything's here: preserving your voice; when and how to use a microphone;
projection; varying pace and pitch ... essential reading."
The Times Educational Supplement

Published by:
Management Pocketbooks Ltd
Laurel House, Station Approach, Alresford, Hants SO24 9JH, U.K.
Tel: +44 (0)1962 735573   Fax: +44 (0)1962 733637
E-mail: sales@pocketbook.co.uk
Website: www.pocketbook.co.uk

This edition published 2004. Reprinted 2006, 2009.

© Richard Payne 2004.

British Library Cataloguing-in-Publication Data – A catalogue record for this book is available from the British Library.

ISBN 978 1 903776 17 9

Design, typesetting and graphics by **efex ltd**. Printed in U.K.

CONTENTS

YOUR VOICE

ABOUT THIS BOOK

The voice is the primary means of communication yet we rarely think about the sound we make until there is a need to speak in public. This book describes the core skills needed to use the voice with confidence and clarity, concentrating on the essential techniques necessary to develop an effective vocal image.

The focus is primarily on presentations and teaching, rather than conversational speech, and is particularly relevant for business presenters, teachers, lecturers, professional speakers and trainers. The term 'audience' in this book refers to those listening to a presentation, pupils in a classroom, and students/delegates on training courses.

Technical jargon has been kept to a minimum and the aim is to provide structured advice and quick tips to help overcome common concerns and problems. There are numerous exercises which you can practise at your own pace, without this being too time-consuming. Finally, the book explains how to look after and maintain your voice, and when you might need to consult a doctor.

FACTORS AFFECTING THE VOICE

There are four factors which influence the way we use our voices when presenting or teaching. We have more control over some of these factors than others.

1. The environment – key considerations

- How large is the audience?
- How is the room/classroom/training room laid out?
- What equipment is available?
- How far away is the audience from the speaking area?
- What are the acoustic properties/characteristics of the room?

FACTORS AFFECTING THE VOICE

1. The environment – tips

- If you are speaking in a large space, use a microphone if you can
- Stand up so that everyone can see you and so you can produce your voice effectively
- Ask the audience to fill up from the front so that any empty seats are at the back (this will reduce the amount of effort needed)
- The acoustic properties of a room depend on the shape, size and materials of the items that enclose and furnish it. If the space produces echoes then slow down to avoid competing with yourself
- Heavily furnished spaces with low ceilings can absorb the voice so you will need to work harder
- The bodies of your audience will also absorb some of the sound
- Breath control, posture and clarity are crucial (see sections on Being Heard, How Your Voice Works and Clarity in Speech)

FACTORS AFFECTING THE VOICE

2. The demand – key considerations

- How frequently are you required to speak, present or teach?
- For how long will you need to speak?

Tips

- If you have a heavy speaking schedule, try to create time to rest your voice between presentations or lessons. For teachers this may not always be possible; therefore ensure you rest your voice in the evenings and at weekends (see *Special Considerations for Classroom Teachers* pages 92 and 93)

- If you need to speak uninterrupted for more than ten minutes then take small sips of water to ensure your throat does not become dry

- Be aware that you need to pause for breath and for the audience to absorb the points being made (see *Why You Should Pause* pages 57 and 58)

- If there is a lot of background noise or the acoustics are poor, consider using amplification, if available

FACTORS AFFECTING THE VOICE

3. Personal resources – key considerations

The following elements have an effect on your voice:

- Your own physiology
- Your gender and age
- Your previous experience
- Your health
- Motivation to communicate clearly
- Your past experiences of using your voice in public

FACTORS AFFECTING THE VOICE

3. Personal resources – tips

- Be aware that your life stage, health and the ageing process affect your vocal mechanism

- Don't take on too much and do pace your speaking engagements so you can recover and rest. (If you are a classroom teacher or lecturer this may not be possible so see *Special Considerations for Classroom Teachers* on pages 92 and 93)

- Use a variety of media in your presentation – do not just rely on the spoken word to communicate (audiences/classes retain more if a variety of media are used)

- Stay as fit as possible. Exercise that is primarily cardiovascular (eg swimming, brisk walking, cycling, running) will help you to develop your breathing. You may prefer yoga or meditation, both of which focus on breathing

FACTORS AFFECTING THE VOICE

4. Technique – key considerations

- Good vocal technique is critical when using the voice. Poor vocal technique can create problems or strain
- It is essential that you look after your voice and care for it. Good habits are crucial, as is avoiding or minimising your exposure to unhealthy environments
- Practise – your voice will not improve unless you commit to developing it

Tips

- Take some lessons from a voice teacher
- Look after your voice (follow the voice care advice in this pocketbook)
- Put time aside to practise the techniques outlined in this book (see pages 95-98)
- Your voice *will* improve if you make a commitment to its development

YOUR VOICE

WHAT MAKES AN EFFECTIVE VOICE?

An effective voice is a combination of:

Vitality   The technical terms for this include modulation and prosody

Audibility   A combination of an appropriate level of volume and the skills of projection

Clarity   Producing a vital audible sound which is distinct
and clear *not* muffled or mumbled

Exercise 1

Take a reading of approximately 200 words. Read through it silently and then aloud as if you were trying to speak to someone sitting next to you. Repeat the reading standing up and imagine you are communicating to fifty people in a large space. As the demand progressively increases ensure that the vitality, audibility and clarity are also increased. Note the particular challenges the exercise presents for you.

HOW THE VOICE COMPLEMENTS THE COMMUNICATION PROCESS

'I do not much dislike the matter, but the manner of his speech.'
Antony and Cleopatra by William Shakespeare.

The way in which you say something can have as much impact on the audience/class as the actual words themselves.

The basic elements of human communication are:

Body language The means of conveying information through gestures, bodily movement or facial expressions

Proxemics The distance maintained between people during interaction

Paralanguage All the things which go alongside our language system and structure which are primarily vocal rather than verbal

HOW THE VOICE COMPLEMENTS THE COMMUNICATION PROCESS

Exercise 2

Think about someone you speak to on the telephone but have not met. Write down the impression you have created of this person. Identify why you might have created such an impression.

If you meet the person compare your impression with the reality. How far apart are the two? When we only have the voice on which to rely we create a mental image of someone based solely on their voice. This mental picture is often inaccurate.

YOUR VOICE

WHY THE SPOKEN WORD DIFFERS FROM THE WRITTEN WORD

Written documents have their own rules of structure, with sections, headings and sub-headings. Sentences are subdivided into clauses and sub-clauses, punctuated by commas, semicolons, colons, brackets and dashes. If you read a report aloud you may find it difficult to follow the printed punctuation and, therefore, add your own micro pauses either for effect or because you need to breathe. Longer written sentences may just be too long to vocalise on one breath.

Linguists use different references for units of speech. Here are some of the more common units of speech:

A spoken discourse: any act of speech which occurs in a given place within a given period of time, eg a presentation, lecture, lesson.

An utterance: a spoken discourse consists of at least one utterance which is a stretch of speech produced by an individual with silence before and after, eg *I think it is going to rain.*

A tone unit: a phrase or group of words which may or may not correspond with the written sentence format. It is the way in which we break up a sentence/clause to make it suitable for spoken communication. A speaker will usually pause between tone units.

HOW YOUR VOICE WORKS

THE ACT OF SPEECH

The production of the human voice is a complex and amazing physical feat. When we speak we can either make a sound or form a word. The production of sound requires the following elements:

An excitor or energiser – in the human mechanism it is the force of the lung air passing up the trachea (wind pipe) and entering the larynx (voice box) which provides energy.

A vocaliser – is formed by your vocal cords which create the primary vibration.

A resonator – resonance enriches the sound we make. The human body has a number of partially filled air cavities where resonance takes place. The vocal tract containing the pharynx, the nasal cavity and the oral cavity can be shaped in various ways to create different resonance chambers.

Note: The space in which you speak also possesses resonating characteristics which may prove a help or a hindrance. It is therefore helpful to familiarize yourself in advance with the space in which you will be working.

THE ACT OF SPEECH

Exercise 3

Take the vowel sound **AH** (as in c<u>ar</u>) and produce it for the count of about six. Start with the jaw almost shut and gradually open the mouth as you produce the **AH** sound. Notice the difference in sound quality. When the mouth is open the sound should be more resonant. The main reason for this is because you have changed the shape of the resonating chamber.

HOW YOUR VOICE WORKS

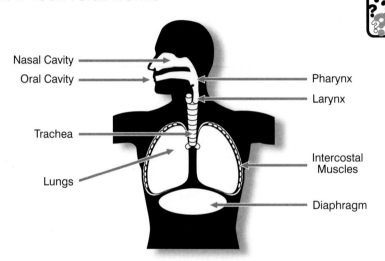

Nasal Cavity

Oral Cavity

Pharynx

Larynx

Trachea

Intercostal Muscles

Lungs

Diaphragm

Diagram of the speaking process.

VOICE PRODUCTION

Before we make a sound it is extremely important to ensure that we stand appropriately.

The **POP** principle will help you:

Posture – you should stand upright and avoid slouching (more specific advice follows).

Orientation – always face the direction in which you want the sound to travel, ie orientate yourself towards the audience/class. A useful guide is to ensure that your feet are pointed towards your audience and not towards the projector screen, chalkboard or the side walls. If you need to write on a chalkboard, wipeboard or flipchart remember to **touch** (write on the board) **turn** (towards the class) then **talk**. Do not write and talk at the same time!

Proxemics – stand as close to your audience/class as possible. However, you should never stand any nearer than arm's length to those sitting in the front row.

YOUR POSTURE IS CRUCIAL

Why?
If your posture is perfect you will find it easier to manage your breath. Your breathing muscles won't be constricted and you will look more confident!

Tips for perfect posture
- Keep feet slightly apart and in contact with the floor
- Distribute weight evenly
- Don't stand with legs crossed, even if behind a lectern (bad for circulation and your torso may become misaligned)
- Keep knees slightly bent to help avoid backache and reduce tension
- Stand tall. Imagine a line running from your belly button up the middle of your body and towards the ceiling. Follow that line with the crown of your skull
- Keep chin parallel to floor – best position for your vocal mechanism when speaking and you will be facing your audience
- Watch shoulders don't carry too much tension. The gentle rise and fall of the shoulders is a natural part of the breathing process but don't *over-use* your shoulders for breathing

YOUR POSTURE IS CRUCIAL

SPEAKING FROM A SEATED POSITION

If you have to speak from a seated position your posture is just as important.
A lot of the tips for perfect posture also apply when you are sitting:

- Do not sit too near or too far away from the table
- Keep your feet in contact with the floor
- Do not cross your legs
- Sit tall
- Ensure the shoulders do not lead the breathing or become fixed at the top of the *in* breath
- Do not perch on the edge of the seat
- Place your lower back against the back of the seat and then lean forwards slightly
- Keep your chin parallel to the table-top when you are speaking
- Do not fidget
- Do not sit on your hands or grip the arms of the chair
- Place your hands on the table in front of you

YOUR POSTURE IS CRUCIAL

FREQUENTLY ASKED QUESTIONS

Q *How can I keep my head up if I need to refer to notes?*

A You can refer to notes. When you drop your head to refresh your memory, simply stop speaking; when you are ready, bring up your head and eyes and resume speaking.

Q *What if I need to turn around to look at the projector screen or to write on the board/flipchart?*

A No problem. Again, turn and look but stop speaking. When you have your prompt, re-orientate yourself, bring your head up and resume speaking. If you are using a computer generated presentation the slide may be on the computer screen in front of you, so you may not need to turn around. If you are using an OHP then the slide will be on the projector in front of you – in which case, look down instead of turning around!

If you are writing on the flipchart, chalkboard or wipeboard remember the **touch, turn, talk** principle (see page 21).

YOUR POSTURE IS CRUCIAL

FREQUENTLY ASKED QUESTIONS

Q *Do I have to stand still in one position when I am speaking?*

A No. You will find that you may start slouching or that your shoulders accumulate tension, ie you are out of alignment, but this isn't a problem – simply re-set yourself. It is not natural to stand completely still. Our bodies make micro movements (this is partly to keep the blood circulating efficiently). Go with the flow. However, you should **not** be in constant motion, eg dancing on the spot or constantly hopping from one foot to the other.

Q *What about moving around the speaking area?*

A Movement is great. It adds visual interest, energises your presentation and helps to provide cues at transition points.

MOVEMENT

GOLDEN RULES

- Do not pace around
- Always move for a reason
- Try to restrict expansive movements to major points of transition in your presentation or lesson, eg when you move from one module/major point to another
- Move from a still position and resume stillness before you move again
- Make the majority of your movements on a horizontal plane (from stage left to stage right) rather than on a vertical plane (from a centre stage or down stage position to an upstage position)
- If you do move on a vertical plane be aware you will need to turn your back on the audience to move upstage (unless you walk backwards!) so stop speaking until you have reached your next point and make sure you turn around before speaking again

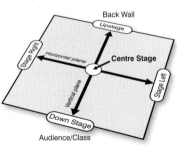

AVOID FIXING OR COLLAPSING

As you breathe in and out and begin to speak it is crucial that you maintain perfect posture.

You must avoid fixing at the top of the *in breath* (inspiration)…

…and collapsing on the *out breath* as you speak (expiration).

Maintain a long back and wide shoulders, and do not hold tension in the shoulders as you breathe.

Result: you will find breathing for speech easier and you will look more confident!

HOW YOUR VOICE WORKS

BREATHING FOR SPEECH

Dispelling some myths about breathing for speech:

- You will find breathing for speech much easier if you spend a little time focusing on your posture

- You do not need to be taught to breathe – you are already an expert!

- When you are presenting or teaching, the physical demand is greater than it is for conversational speech

- During a presentation or lecture you will need to take bigger breaths more frequently

- Because of this requirement, you will find it easier to control the breath if you slow down your rate of delivery by pausing more often and for longer. Think of these pauses as your opportunities to refuel

BREATHING FOR SPEECH

You need to develop and control your breathing when teaching or presenting. When you take a controlled big breath you can use your three lower pairs of ribs which are attached indirectly to the sternum by cartilage and, therefore, have more scope for all-round movement.

When you take a deep breath your lower ribs swing outwards and upwards and increase the size of the chest. Breath is drawn into the lungs.

The diaphragm muscle is also involved in this process. You can neither feel nor touch this muscle but it separates the thorax from the abdomen. As you breathe in, the rib-cage expands outwards, the diaphragm contracts, enlarging the cavity of the chest from top to bottom.

Your abdominal muscles also help to support the breathing process.

To ensure your diaphragm, abdominal and intercostal muscles are not constricted, focus on your posture.

BREATH MANAGEMENT

Exercise 4

To ensure you are taking in enough air and to feel the movement of the lower ribs, start by tracing the line of the lowest rib you can feel from your breastbone to your spine.

Bear in mind that these ribs are not actually our lowest ribs. We also have two unattached ribs which are joined only at the spine but it can be a little difficult to locate these when standing.

Exercise 5

Place your forefinger as near as you can to the lowest part of the breastbone. Follow the line of your lowest rib with the thumb as far back towards the spine as you can.

Stand tall and wide, preferably in front of a full-length mirror. Breathe in slowly and deeply for the count of three and then breathe out for as long as you wish. Repeat this three times. You should be able to feel the full expansion of the lower ribs. If you cannot feel any rib movement then take slightly bigger breaths.

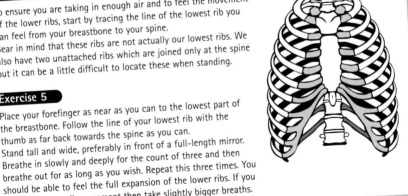

BREATH MANAGEMENT

CONNECTING THE BREATH WITH THE VOICE

The following exercise will start the process of connecting the breath stream with the voice.

Exercise 6

1. Stand tall and wide (remember to keep your head up).
2. Breathe in for the count of three.
3. Pause very briefly.
4. Count aloud from one to eight on one breath and concentrate on maintaining your posture and controlling an even flow of breath.
5. Try to avoid 'fixing' or 'collapsing'.

Congratulations! You have just learned how to: maintain your posture, avoid fixing or collapsing and control your breath.

It is no more complicated than that!

BREATH MANAGEMENT

CONNECTING THE BREATH WITH THE VOICE

When you start to speak you should always have enough breath to get you through the first phrase.

As soon as you feel you are reaching the end of your breath stream, pause and take another breath to get you to the end of the next tone unit (see page 16 for definition). Do not try to carry on speaking!

Remember you need deeper breaths for teaching/presenting than you do for conversational speech.

BEING HEARD

VOLUME AND PROJECTION

Volume and projection are interrelated but they are not the same thing.

Volume is a variable aspect of speech, ie we can choose to speak in a low volume (such as a whisper) or we can choose to use a high level of volume. Most of the time volume is related to pitch as well:

- The lower the volume – the lower the pitch
- The higher the volume – the higher the pitch

Projection enables the receiver of a spoken discourse to decode the message without having to strain; therefore we should always project our voice. It is possible to project the voice using a low level of volume (eg a whisper) or a high level of volume. Projection is not about shouting or causing vocal strain, nor is it about producing so much volume that your audience or class flinch.

EFFECTIVE PROJECTION

In order for you to project the voice effectively the following things need to be present:

- Clear vowel and consonant production
- Release of the voice into the space
- Appropriate positioning (orientation)
- Breath support
- Appropriate posture
- Effective pacing

BEING HEARD

PROJECTION IN THE CLASSROOM/TRAINING ROOM/LECTURE THEATRE

Classrooms can be noisy. Constant shouting to gain attention or settle the class is best avoided. Try to use other non-verbal cues to gain attention, eg gesture, visual aids, pre-recorded sound.

Your aim as a teacher is to allow your students to hear you comfortably without having to lean forward in their seats or draw back because of excessive volume.

Attempt to use a well-projected voice, with a high level of volume only for short periods in order to settle the class down. Reduce the volume as soon as the background noise diminishes. Some teachers speak at an unnecessarily high level of volume to discourage further noise during a lesson. Better to deal with such an event if it arises as it will mean less sustained effort is needed throughout the lesson.

Plan voice rests into your lessons. No lesson should consist entirely of teacher talk. A variety of teaching methods should be used. By giving work to your students or pupils you can have a short rest.

PROJECTION EXERCISE

Exercise 7

1. Stand in alignment.
2. Place your hand about an arm's length away from your face.
3. Breathe out and direct the breath without strain towards the hand. You may even be able to feel the breath on your hand.
4. Choose a short sentence which you are able to get through on one breath, perhaps from the start of your lesson/presentation.
5. Put your hand down and choose a point about two metres away. Breathe out towards this point and repeat the sentence concentrating on directing it to this point.
6. Choose another point about five metres away and repeat as before, starting with the breath and then using your practice sentence.

VOLUME AND PROJECTION
TARGET THE VOICE

- Orientate yourself so you are always facing the audience when you speak
- Stand as close as possible to your target audience
- Stand tall and wide
- Keep your chin parallel to the floor when speaking
- Start each tone unit on a full breath
- Pause for breath when necessary – never speak on the end of a breath stream
- Speak a little slower than you would in conversational speech – do not gabble
- Open your mouth a little wider than you would usually
- Ensure you fully form all your words
- Watch the consonants, particularly when they appear at the ends of words. They can sometimes be weakly pronounced
- Exaggerate your consonant production a little

BEING HEARD

EXPLORING THE RELATIONSHIP BETWEEN VOLUME AND PROJECTION

This exercise should be undertaken standing, and preferably in front of a mirror so you are able to monitor your progress. The aim is to ensure that all the prerequisites for projection are present as you vary the volume.

Exercise 8

Say this aloud relatively slowly. Remember to pause for breath whenever you need to. You may wish to breathe at the commas.

To sit in solemn silence in a dull dark dock,
In a pestilential prison with a life-long lock,
Awaiting the sensation of a short sharp shock
From a cheap and chippy chopper on a big black block.

Say it once through in a whisper and then
   just below your normal speaking voice and then
      at the normal level you would use for a conversation and then
         the level that would be appropriate for a presentation to approx. fifty people and finally
            a high level of volume (not a shout)

BEING HEARD

EXPLORING THE RELATIONSHIP BETWEEN VOLUME AND PROJECTION

LEARNING POINTS AND TIPS

You may need to copy out the reading (on the previous page) and paste it up at eye level so you are able to keep your head up.

In a whisper the vocal chords are wide apart (in fact, there is no voice), offering little resistance to the breath stream. Therefore, you need lots of breath and you also need to produce your consonants clearly otherwise the sound will be unclear.

You will also use a lot of breath when you are using a high level of volume.

You should aim to get through Exercise 8 without any tension or strain in your throat or neck.

VARIETY IN SPEECH

WHY IS VARIETY IMPORTANT?

- Monotonous voices can be boring to listen to
- Your audience/students may stop listening if your voice is monotonous
- You will not sound committed to your subject if there is no energy in the delivery

VARIETY IN SPEECH

THE ESSENTIAL ELEMENTS

A voice with variety contains a combination of the following elements:

- **Pitch** – a variety of notes and intonations
- **Appropriate pace** – the speed at which we speak
- **Pauses** – these break up our speech and can assist in the process of providing an interesting sound. Pauses provide rhythm to our delivery
- **Volume** – a variety of volume levels helps to create an atmosphere
- **Word emphasis** – emphasizing words can be a powerful way of instilling energy into the delivery

YOUR AIM

Work on **one** of these essential elements at a time.

Do not attempt too much otherwise it will be overwhelming.

Remember!

- You will already be using a lot of these techniques in your conversational speech
- For presenting/teaching, some of these techniques need to be enlarged or exaggerated
- It is quite natural to feel a little self-conscious at first when you are trying out these new approaches
- Persevere: constant practice is the only way to improve!

VARIETY IN SPEECH

PITCH

Pitch is the note or notes which we use when we speak. The human speaking voice has a range of between 5-8 available notes.

The pitch range is the difference between our lowest and our highest note:
- The male pitch range is generally lower than the female pitch range
- Our modal pitch is the term used to describe the habitual note we strike
- Some people strike a note and do not move from that note, which results in monotonous speech

Exercise 9

Say the following statement aloud:
My father's bought a new car.

Now repeat as a question:
My father's bought a new car?

This demonstrates the pitch changes you produce when making a statement compared to asking a question.

PITCH RANGE

The reason for the difference in pitch range is connected with gender. A man's vocal cords are approximately 30mm long, while a woman's vocal cords are approximately 20mm long. The man's longer vocal cords vibrate slower and give a deeper voice.

When the vocal cords are wide open they vibrate slowly, creating a low pitch sound.

When the vocal cords are close together, they vibrate rapidly to create a high pitch sound.

When we speak we rarely make a step change from one pitch to another. It is more normal to glide momentarily into a note slightly above or slightly below our starting note and then to return to that starting note.

Problems can arise when your starting note is in your upper range, as it can make the voice seem thin and reedy or give a frivolous quality to what you say.

Pitch glides can occur anywhere in a tone unit, but for formal speech it is best to restrict **major** pitch glides to the start of a tone unit or the end.

VARIETY IN SPEECH

INTONATION

Pitch is sometimes referred to as intonation. Here are four of the most common intonation sounds:

- **Long fall** which suggests finality, confidence – when you wish to say something and have no intention of adding to it and you do not expect a response, eg:

  'I think the sun's coming ⬇ out'

- **Short fall** which suggests abrupt termination. You may give the impression you are busy or do not wish to be bothered, eg:

  Request: 'Can you finish this work before leaving tonight?'
  Reply: ➘ 'Yes'

Key	
⬇ Long fall	➘ Short fall

VARIETY IN SPEECH

INTONATION

- **Long rise** which suggests a desire for a reply. This is typically used when asking for a *yes* or *no* response, ie a question which does not begin with the words who, where, when, what, how, why. Eg:

  'This is a *test?'*

- **Short rise** – used, for example, when trying to attract someone's attention or when replying if someone tries to get our attention:

  Question: *'Fred?'*

  Reply:  *'Yes'*

Key	
⬆ Long rise	⬈ Short rise

Some conventional uses of pitch:

- The readers of classified football results in the United Kingdom use changes in pitch/intonation to indicate the score
- Newsreaders will often change the pitch at the onset of a new story

PITCH AND MOOD

Pitch can also indicate mood.

For example:

- A sustained period of speech in a *high pitch* can indicate sarcasm, lightheartedness or tension

- A sustained period of speech in a *lower pitch* indicates seriousness and gravity

Note how newsreaders will use a higher pitch for the more humorous stories and a lower pitch for more serious stories.

PITCH: EXERCISE

Exercise 10

Listed on the following page are the eight elements necessary to make the perfect cup of tea.

- Read through the list, adding a few words of instruction to each item (as a qualifying statement) before moving on to the next item
- Try to ensure you are on your central note to start
- Try at least one momentary glide **above** your central note, near the start of one of the items
- Try at least one momentary glide **below** your central note, near the start of one of the items

In other words, during your short speech you should have used: your central note, one glide **above** your central note and one glide **below** your central note.
Practise on your own to start with because it is quite natural to feel a little self-conscious when rehearsing this technique at first.

PITCH: EXERCISE

Exercise 10 (continued)

Elements for making the perfect cup of tea:

1. Teabag
2. Teapot
3. Water
4. Kettle
5. Cup
6. Milk
7. Sugar
8. Spoon

Don't forget to add your own instructions to qualify each item on the list, eg *Take one teabag for each person. Place in the teapot* etc....

Notice, as you practise your speech, how the changes in pitch add variety and interest.

....and pour!

51

VARIETY IN SPEECH

PACE

- Pace is the speed at which we speak
- Pace can be expressed in words per minute (WPM)
- Conversational speech can take place as rapidly as 180-200 WPM
- 200 WPM is too fast for presentations, speeches, lectures or lessons
- You should aim to speak at between 120-150 WPM

Speaking at a constant rate is not recommended as this would be somewhat monotonous. Variety in pace is important.

Sometimes you may speak slightly above the recommended rate and sometimes you may speak slightly below to provide variety for your audience.

You should not speak at a fast rate for a sustained period, particularly when teaching.

PACE

Most people speak far too quickly when they present or teach. It is rare for people to speak too slowly. People speak quickly because they are nervous and they wish to get through the ordeal as soon as possible.

If you speak too quickly you will gabble and some of your words will be unclear. You will have less time to articulate. You may lose control of your breathing and posture.

If your audience wants to make notes or you are explaining new or difficult concepts, speaking too rapidly can mean people 'tune out' or stop listening.

The key message for most of us is to **SLOW DOWN**.

PACE

HOW TO SLOW DOWN

Unlike singers who can stretch out a note or a word (usually on a vowel sound), speakers cannot do this without the resulting sound appearing strange or unusual to the audience.

The only option you have is to **increase the lengths and incidents of pauses and to take care producing the consonants.**

PACE: EXERCISE

Exercise 11

Read the following at your natural rate and time yourself:

A good speech is one which is memorable. A good speech is usually not too long. One of the greatest virtues a speaker can possess is brevity.

This begs the question, how does one go about constructing and delivering an address to an audience?

There are some basic principles which should be observed. Firstly, never speak on a subject about which you know nothing or are in any way unsure. Secondly, do not be tempted to give an impromptu speech until you are very experienced and thirdly, try not to make too many points.

Finally, remember rehearsal is also extremely important. Many top speakers spend hours practising their delivery and this is time well spent. Paying particular attention to the voice is good advice because if you are not used to speaking in public then you will need to establish how to project and produce your voice effectively.

(148 words)

PACE: EXERCISE

Exercise 11 (continued)

If you have finished the reading on the previous page before one minute has elapsed, then you are probably speaking too quickly.

Set a minute on your watch or a timer, and repeat the reading. Try to slow down, ensuring the reading lasts for approximately one minute.

If you succeed in achieving this, then you should bear in mind that this is about the rate at which you need to be speaking when presenting or teaching.

PAUSES

Pauses can be frightening.
A pause is silence.
Speakers often feel that a pause during a
presentation is a sign of weakness.
In fact, a pause can project confidence.

Why you should pause:

- To breathe. As we have previously discovered,
  breathing is crucial to voice production and
  phrasing
- For effect. You may wish to give students/audience
  members time to consider a point you have made
- After you have asked a question. When you ask a
  question, do not be frightened to pause for quite
  some time in order to encourage responses
- Before you answer a question. If your answer is
  extremely important then pausing briefly makes your
  answer seem considered

VARIETY IN SPEECH

PAUSES

Why you should pause (cont'd):

- When you are introducing visual aids. This provides time for the audience to take in and process the visual image. It will also ensure the visual aid has increased impact

- When you turn away or look down. It is crucial that you do not speak with your head facing towards your notes or the screen. Pause if you look down or turn away

- Your audience needs time to think about what you have said. Some of the information may be new to them. A pause allows them this time

- Your pupils/students or audience may wish to make notes. Note-taking should be encouraged, particularly in learning environments. Frequent pauses allow those making notes time to catch up

PAUSES: EXERCISE

Exercise 12

Make two copies of the reading on page 55 (keep the second copy for Exercise 14). Read it aloud a few times and mark in where you think you should pause.

There are two sorts of pauses:
- **Phrasing pauses** are short and break up a longer sentence into manageable chunks for speech, represented by /
- **Punctuation pauses** are longer and usually occur at punctuation marks (eg full stops), represented by //

Read it again and when you come to a phrasing pause, count one beat before you start speaking again. Make the punctuation pauses longer. Don't forget to take a breath during some of the pauses!

A good speech / is one which is memorable.// A good speech / is usually not too long.// One of the greatest virtues a speaker can possess / is brevity.//

Remember, what seems like a long pause to you will seem like a natural break for the audience and will also give them time to think about what you have said.

VARIETY IN SPEECH

VOLUME

We have already looked at varying the volume (page 39); however, bear in mind that you can use variety in volume during a talk or presentation to create a mood or atmosphere or to add weight to what you are saying.

Exercise 13

- Take text of approximately 150-200 words, perhaps from a book or newspaper
- Identify in advance at least three places where you feel you could vary the volume
- Practise the reading three times with the variations

  Do not make the changes too dramatic or you will feel self-conscious!

WORD EMPHASIS

In any tone unit or phrase certain words will have more importance. In order to highlight the importance of such words we use **emphasis**. There are no strict rules about which words to emphasize.

Why use word emphasis?

- Provides added weight
- Aids variety
- It is a popular convention
- Helps you identify important words

Bear in mind we also emphasize individual syllables in words containing more than one syllable. This is an extremely technical and complicated aspect of language and pronunciation, so we will concentrate on whole-word emphasis.

WORD EMPHASIS

What do we do when we emphasize a word?

When emphasizing a single word we usually:

- Pause very briefly before the word (a micro pause)
- Give the word weight and attack (attack = a small increase in volume)

We may also change the pitch or inflection of the word.

For a formal speech we need to give emphasized words a little more attack than we would in conversational speech. Think of these as high value words.

Be careful not to give the words too much attack or to pause for too long, otherwise the result will sound stilted and unnatural.

VARIETY IN SPEECH

WORD EMPHASIS

Exercise 14

Take your second copy of the reading* on page 55. Divide it up into tone units or phrases. Highlight or underline one word in each phrase.

Practise the reading, concentrating on ensuring you emphasize the high value words you have highlighted.

Exercise 15 (advanced)

As above, but ask someone to assist:

- Provide them with an unmarked copy of the reading
- Do not show them the words you have decided to emphasize
- Ask them to underline the words they hear emphasized when you read
- Compare their copy with your marked one – the underlined or highlighted words should be identical

*You can, of course, use your own reading if you wish.

VARIETY IN SPEECH

RECAP EXERCISE

Exercise 16

- Identify one aspect of vocal skills that you have worked on so far
- Select an extract from a talk, lesson or presentation you have previously given, or are about to give, and record it or ask someone else to listen to it
- If you have recorded it, play it back to yourself and concentrate on evaluating the aspect of vocal skills on which you have chosen to work

 Nobody likes the sound of their own voice when it is played back. If you really cannot bear to hear your own voice, then instead of recording it ask someone to listen to your talk and provide you with feedback.

CLARITY IN SPEECH

SUSTAINING VOCAL ENERGY THROUGHOUT A PHRASE

Sometimes people start a phrase with the right amount of energy and then fade away ….

This results in the latter part of the phrase becoming mumbled, indistinct and unclear. It can also mean that vital information is missed.

Most of the time this results from:

- Habit
- Poor breath management
- People 'forward gaining' or thinking about what they are going to say next
- Poor phrasing (see next page)

CLARITY IN SPEECH

SUSTAINING VOCAL ENERGY THROUGHOUT A PHRASE

Exercise 17

Try this sentence on one breath without a pause:

'People often worry about going blank or forgetting what comes next and this is perfectly understandable.'

You may feel uncomfortable trying to get through this on one breath and, as a consequence, fade away slightly. Better to think about splitting it up or phrasing it appropriately.

Try again. Ensure you pause briefly and take a breath at the forward slashes:

'People often worry about going blank / or forgetting what comes next / and this is perfectly understandable.'

You will probably find that by phrasing it appropriately you will manage your breath and ensure that the energy is sustained throughout the sentence. In addition, none of the vital information is omitted.

WHY CLEAR SPEECH IS IMPORTANT

- Clear speech is one of the prerequisites of projecting the voice

- There is little point producing a vital sound if it is muffled or indistinct

- When you are presenting information, clarity is crucial because the listener does not usually have a chance to stop you for clarification

THE NATURE OF SPEECH

- Speech is the result of resonance, obstruction or both together
- Vowels are pure resonance and are carried on the breath stream
- Vowel quality depends on what part of the tongue is raised, how high it is raised and whether the lips are rounded and therefore pushed forwards
- Consonants are produced by some form of barrier or obstruction to the breath stream

69

CLARITY IN SPEECH

MAXIMUM IMPACT WITH MINIMUM EFFORT

It is estimated that conversational speech is formed at approximately five syllables per second! It is impossible to think about each shape and sound you make. The trick is to ensure that the basic predispositions for clear speech are present.

The essential elements:

- Ensure the jaw is nice and relaxed
- If you hold tension in the jaw, then have a yawn, as this is the best exercise to relax the jaw and the throat
- Keep the consonants as light and precise as possible

Exercise 18

Count aloud from one to ten and concentrate on ensuring that your jaw is relaxed and that you keep the consonants precise but light.

CLARITY IN SPEECH

VOWELS

There are only six written symbols for the vowel sounds in written English and these are (a e i o u y). Note that y is used to represent a consonant as well. There are an amazing number of variations produced from these six vowel sounds alone.

Vowels can be classified as:

- **Simple vowels** – eg in the word *of* or *as*

- **Compound vowels** – where one vowel sound flows directly to another, eg as in the words *now, player*

Each simple vowel has its own shape which is created by the tongue, the lips and the cheeks, and as long as you sustain the vowel sound that shape does not change.

Resonance takes place predominantly in the mouth and throat.

CLARITY IN SPEECH

VOWELS

TIPS FOR VOWEL PRODUCTION

- Keep the teeth a consistent distance apart – as a guide a thumb's width
- The tongue can rest behind the bottom teeth for all vowel production
- The lips should be well rounded

Exercise 19 – vowel chain

Practise this exercise concentrating on clear vowel production.
Try the words first and then just isolate the vowels.

How – ow	Pie – eye	A – a	Making – ay
To – oo	And – a	Lawyer – aw y er	Their – air
Bake – ay	It – i	On – o	Fierce – ear
Bad – a	Needs – ee	Fire – eye er	Noise – oy!

Repeat this exercise on a regular basis.

CONSONANTS

A consonant is any speech sound made with an obstruction of the air stream. This process is called articulation. When we articulate we can describe the shape we make with our mouth by identifying four things:

Thhhhh

1. The manner of articulation, ie how we articulate.

2. The articulator and the place of articulation, ie which two parts of the speaking mechanism come into contact.

3. Whether the vocal cords are moving or vibrating (this is known as voicing).

4. The shape of the tongue and lips.

CONSONANTS

Articulation happens when an articulator comes into contact with a point of articulation.

The main articulators in the human body used for speech are:

- The lower lip (we need the lower lip to make an F or V sound)
- The different parts of the tongue

The main points of articulation in the human body which are used for speech are:

- The upper lip
- The upper front teeth
- The terrace-like structure behind the upper teeth
- The hard palate
- The soft palate (the part of the roof of the mouth that has no bone above it)
- The wall of the pharynx

IMPROVING CLARITY

The consonants chop up the voice stream and help to give it definition by creating separations between the vowel sounds. This, in conjunction with syllables, gives the rhythm and energy to our units of speech.

Tips

- Don't speak too quickly as you will have less time to articulate

- Ensure that any contact is clean and precise but not violent

- Focus in particular on clear consonant production when they appear on the ends of words

- Focus particularly on producing clear final *T* sounds, eg *It, print, quaint, dust*

A WORD ABOUT OVER ARTICULATION OR CLIPPED SPEECH

Any speaking technique can be both exaggerated and abused so that the resulting sound appears absurd or unnatural. The key is to get the right balance between clarity and a natural sound.

In conversational speech you might neutralise some of the vowels and consonants.
'I'd like a cup of tea and a pint of beer' might be spoken like this:

'I'd like u cup 'v tea 'nd a pine 'v beer'

You don't want to produce and enunciate every sound with an over-exaggerated clarity, nor should you use your everyday approach. The trick is to modify your conversational approach whilst keeping some of its naturalness and rhythm.

EXAMPLES OF SOME CONSONANT TYPES

The classification of our vowels and consonants is a complex and time-consuming activity. Below are just a few examples of consonant types with which you can practise.

Exercise 20

Try to identify how these consonants are made.

F as in five	T as in time	M as in mad
V as in vital	D as in down	
B as in Bob	Th as in this	N as in nun
P as in pop	Th as in thin	

(Answers on page 112)

CLARITY IN SPEECH

CONSONANT SOUNDS

Did you notice that four of the examples in Exercise 20 were in pairs? The reason they were in pairs is that some of our consonant sounds are made in the same way but with one vital difference:

One is voiced, eg *D*
One is unvoiced (there is no sound), eg *T*

Some consonants are referred to as sonorant consonants, meaning that the consonant can be sustained for as long as you have enough breath.

For example:

- The word *Dad* has a consonant on the end of the word which cannot be sustained

- The word *diagram* has a consonant on the end of the word which can be sustained as long as you have a breath stream. The reason for this is that there is nasal resonance

CLARITY IN SPEECH

TIPS FOR THOSE WHO SPEAK ENGLISH AS ANOTHER LANGUAGE

- Don't worry too much about your accent, instead concentrate on clear speech

- Native English speakers are used to hearing their language spoken with a variety of dialects and accents

- Ensure you do not speak too quickly as this can create problems for native listeners/audiences

- Be aware that some consonant sounds in the English language may not exist in other languages. Try to identify these consonants and practise them

- If you are presenting or teaching, then support your oral presentation with visual aids and handouts if you are worried about expressing yourself clearly

- Rehearse a formal presentation beforehand with a native English speaker and ask for feedback on pronunciation

- Listen to native speakers and concentrate on their pronunciation as this will help you to learn

- Undertake the speech clarity exercise (see next page)

ASSESSING YOUR SPEECH CLARITY

Exercise 21

- Take a reading of approximately 300 words
- Read through aloud twice
- Time your reading (**reminder**: your reading should take approximately two minutes. If the reading takes less than two minutes you are speaking too fast so try again and slow down!)
- Read it a third time concentrating on clarity and audio-record this version, if possible
- Play back the recording and assess your speaking clarity, focusing particularly on the consonants
- Ask someone else to listen to the reading and provide you with feedback in relation to clarity

Note: A higher specification of audio recording equipment will provide a more accurate reproduction of the sound you make.

ASSESSING YOUR SPEECH CLARITY

Exercise 22 (for diction)

This reading is quite a challenge! Concentrate on the clear production of consonants, particularly when they appear on the ends of words.

You can record and assess this reading as well if you wish.

Reading

The elegantly appointed room faced out towards the east. The delicacy of the wallpaper added a tasteful and dashing splash of colour to the room distinguished for its quaint collection of bric-a-brac. The couch was an opulent, luxurious left-over from an earlier generation. The clock ticking on the wall magnificently reflected the past passion for pendulums and painted dials. In a corner concealed by curtains a candle of considerable antiquity disintegrated in the dust.

75 words

ASSESSING YOUR SPEECH CLARITY

Additional reading

Houses in twos and threes pass by us, solitary farms, ruinous buildings, dye-works, tanneries and the like, open country, avenues of leafless trees. The hard, uneven pavement is under us, the soft deep mud is on either side. Sometimes we strike into the skirting mud, to avoid the stones that clatter and shake us; sometimes we stick in sloughs and ruts there. The agony of our impatience is then so great that in our wild alarm and hurry we are for getting out and running – hiding – doing anything but stopping.

91 words

MICROPHONE TECHNIQUE

WHAT A MICROPHONE WILL AND WILL NOT DO

A microphone and amplification system will do three things:

1. Amplify your voice.
2. Allow you to speak for prolonged periods with less physical effort.
3. Enable you to enhance or mix the quality of sound by using balance and perhaps one or two basic effects (this would usually require advice from a sound technician).

A microphone will not:

- Make your speech clearer
- Make your voice more vital
- Enable you to produce your voice appropriately for teaching/presenting

Remember the old saying **GIGO**:   Garbage In – Garbage Out

In other words if you put an indistinct flat sound into a microphone, all that the system will do is to amplify that sound!

MICROPHONE TECHNIQUE

WHEN TO USE A MICROPHONE

- In a 'set piece' occasion when everyone else is using one
- In extremely large spaces or lecture theatres
- If you have to deliver a prolonged period of uninterrupted speech in a large space
- Outdoors, in front of a large crowd
- If you have been advised by a doctor or speech therapist to use a microphone to avoid exacerbating an existing condition
- If there is a lot of background noise

MICROPHONE TECHNIQUE

DIFFERENT TYPES OF MICROPHONE

A microphone's job is to convert sound into electrical energy.

An omni-directional microphone picks up sound more or less equally from all directions, including behind the microphone.

A unidirectional microphone picks up most of the sound from the front of the microphone. This helps to reduce unwanted sound from around the microphone.

Microphones can also be:

- **Static**, ie fixed on a stand
- **Clip microphones** – clipped to an item of clothing usually around the upper chest area
- **Radio microphones** – these allow the speaker to move around relatively freely whilst speaking, although they may need to be held by the speaker

TIPS ON USING A MICROPHONE

Good microphone technique will add to your effectiveness as a speaker.

Tips for static microphones:

- Position the microphone as close to the sound source as possible
- Position yourself about six inches away from the microphone head
- If you wish to increase the bass enhancement, get a little closer
- Do not touch the head of the microphone
- Make sure the microphone stand is at the right height for you. If it is not, adjust it before you start to speak (preferably with the microphone turned off)
- Before you start to speak check whether or not there is a switch on the microphone. If there is, ensure it is in the *on* position

TIPS ON USING A MICROPHONE

Tips for static microphones (cont'd):

- Ensure that the microphone head is pointing in the direction of your mouth. If not adjust it (preferably with the microphone turned off)

- Feedback is your enemy, so ensure the speakers are as far away to the sides of the room as possible

- Be sure that the microphone is pointed towards the speaker and away from the loudspeakers

- If you are holding a microphone check that you do not allow your hand to partially cover it

- Practise using microphones before you deliver your presentation!

VOICE CARE AND DEVELOPMENT

LOOKING AFTER YOUR VOICE

If you do a lot of teaching, training or presenting, you need to look after your voice. If you do so it should last a lifetime!

- Practise producing your voice appropriately. Poor technique is the main cause of voice problems

- If you do strain your voice the best advice is to rest it until the next day

- If you have a persistent dry cough then consult a laryngologist

- Try to avoid over-the-counter medicines which promise to dry up mucus. Mucus is necessary to lubricate the larynx

- Smoking can cause cordal damage and in the long-term may affect the ability to control the breath effectively for speech. Take advice about giving up – it is the best thing you can do for your general health and for your voice!

- Dairy products can increase mucus production, so try to reduce your consumption of such foods if you have a heavy speaking schedule

- Avoid smoky environments, if possible

LOOKING AFTER YOUR VOICE

- Alcohol can affect the blood flow to the vocal cords, so avoid drinking before a speech or lesson
- Avoid very noisy social environments as you may strain the voice in order to be heard
- If you are in a noisy environment ask the people or person listening to you to move as near as possible
- Try not to let your mouth or throat become dry when speaking. Take frequent small sips of water
- Avoid drinking carbonated water when presenting as this can cause you to burp!
- If you lose your voice do not be tempted to whisper your way through a presentation or lesson; this can prolong your recovery period or potentially cause damage to the vocal cords

If you have a heavy speaking schedule then make sure you build in rest periods between presentations or lessons – eg ask someone else to take your phone calls, do not shout or cheer and do not go into noisy environments where you may have to speak above a background noise for long periods of time.

SPECIAL CONSIDERATIONS FOR CLASSROOM TEACHERS

Classroom teachers are often powerless to rest their voice but it can be done with a little ingenuity. Some of these tips will also be relevant to trainers and lecturers.

- Build in short rests to your lesson by asking students to undertake an exercise or practical which you are able to supervise without constant 'teacher talk'

- Ensure you rest your voice at break time and at lunchtime, even just for five minutes. Silence and stillness are also beneficial for clearing your mind and de-stressing!

- Use a variety of media during lessons; let someone else take the strain (eg play a video, DVD or sound clip)

- Avoid shouting at pupils over distance in the open air (eg playground or sports field) as there is often a lot of background noise and little environmental resonance, which can lead to added vocal strain. If you need to attract the attention of students when outdoors, move as close as possible before you start to speak. Once you start to address the students instruct them to move closer towards you or ask them to accompany you indoors

SPECIAL CONSIDERATIONS FOR CLASSROOM TEACHERS

- Rest your voice in the evenings and at weekends during term time

- If you catch a cold or flu and have to continue teaching, then inhaling steam from hot (rather than boiling) water is advisable. Adding vapours is unnecessary and there is a risk of drying up mucus membranes

- If you experience persistent problems consult an occupational health professional who may be able to advise on the availability of speech therapy or voice lessons for classroom teachers. Alternatively your GP will advise

- If you are permitted any input into your staff development programme, then consider suggesting a session on vocal technique/voice care

SEEKING MEDICAL ADVICE

Most of the problems speakers experience with their voice can be dealt with by making some form of personal adjustment, eg looking after yourself and ensuring your vocal mechanism is allowed adequate rest. However, there are occasions where you should think about seeking medical advice:

- If you wear dentures (you should ensure they fit well as this can affect the process of articulation and also affect the head, neck and back relationship as you make adjustments or compensate for poorly fitting false teeth)

- If you suffer any severe trauma to the lips, teeth, mouth or throat

- If you suffer from gastroesophageal reflux (this can sometimes affect the throat)

- If you experience a sudden and unexplained loss of voice

- If you have experienced vocal strain or loss of voice and, having rested it, there is no improvement

- If you develop breathing difficulties which may affect your ability to produce the voice adequately for teaching or presenting

VOICE CARE AND DEVELOPMENT

DEVELOPING THE VOICE

To improve your ability to use your voice effectively, you need to commit yourself to developing it:

- Set aside 20 minutes or so each week to practise your posture and breathing technique
- Consider finding out more about yoga and meditation: they both help improve breath control and posture
- Undertake a reading of about 150 words per week and concentrate on clear vowel and consonant production
- Buy a book of fairy tales or children's stories containing a range of characters. Read a few pages a week and concentrate on dramatising the narrative and the characters (develops vocal vitality)
- Listen to others whose voices you admire. Critically evaluate what it is you appreciate about the particular voice
- Find out more about the Alexander Technique* as this will help you to work on your posture
- Take advice from a voice teacher

*The website for The Society of Teachers of The Alexander Technique is www.stat.org.uk

VOICE CARE AND DEVELOPMENT

A PROMISE

Your voice will not improve or develop unless you put some time aside to work on it.

Life is hectic but a 20-30 minute commitment each week should make a noticeable difference in about 2-3 months.

THREE IMPORTANT CONSIDERATIONS WHEN PRACTISING

1. If you are working on your own and doing vocal exercises, ensure you are not going to be interrupted.

2. Work in a space that has good acoustic properties. Do not practise outdoors as this requires a special technique and can place an extra strain on the voice.

3. You will not relax if you are worrying about being overheard, so try and choose a time to practise when there is no one else about!

97

VOICE CARE AND DEVELOPMENT

USING A TAPE/AUDIO RECORDER

Using a tape or audio recorder can be helpful. However, it may also be a hindrance because most people do not like the sound of their own voice!

Most tape recorders will not provide an entirely accurate reproduction of the sound you actually produce.

Audio playback **is** helpful to establish your pacing, speech clarity and your use of emphasis.

If you are going to use a tape recorder or any other form of audio playback then use the highest quality equipment possible as this will give you the most accurate reproduction.

VOICE CARE AND DEVELOPMENT

RELAXING THE THROAT AND NECK

Exercise 23

This exercise should be undertaken prior to speaking:

- Yawn once and then...
- Tip the head backwards gently and **very** slowly
- Yawn with your head in this position
- Bring your head forward into alignment gently and **very** slowly...
- Yawn once more

By now your throat and neck should be completely relaxed!

VOICE CARE AND DEVELOPMENT

RELAXING THE JAW JOINT

The jaw consists of the upper jaw (maxilla) and the lower jaw (mandible).
The lower jaw can move in a sliding direction and up and down (further to and from the upper jaw). Sometimes tension can be present in the muscles needed to move the jaw. The yawning exercise is a good starting point to relax the jaw, but here is a little rhyme which will give your jaw a good workout.

Exercise 24

Undertake this exercise in front of a mirror if you can and exaggerate the vowel sounds to give you the maximum workout:

Here lie the bones of Ida White,
She took life in her stride.
She neither looked to left nor right,
Ignored the guiding traffic light –
I'm not surprised she died.

OTHER KEY CONSIDERATIONS

THE *TH* SOUND

This sound causes particular problems for some speakers whose first language is not English.

There are two sounds represented by *TH*:

- *These* – voiced
- *Thin* – unvoiced

Common faults

- Substituting an F or V – eg *Fick* for *Thick*, *Vose* for *Those*
- Using a D – eg *dis* instead of *this*

How to form the *TH* sound

- The soft palate should be raised to prevent air escaping down the nose
- Place the tongue tip forwards against the upper teeth
- The sides of the tongue will hold the upper side teeth
- Force air between the tongue tip and teeth with an audible friction

THE *TH* SOUND

Exercise 25

Words to practise an unvoiced *TH*:
- Thought thirty three
- Lethal cathedral
- Bath tenth

Words to practise a voiced *TH*:
- This that thither
- Weather mother father
- Smooth

Identify some more words with both of these *TH* sounds, make a list of them, and practise!

OTHER KEY CONSIDERATIONS

TIPS FOR MEETINGS

The key challenge in meetings is to ensure you sound authoritative and that you are able to create space to make your contribution without strain.

- Concentrate on perfect posture as you are likely be seated
- Orientate yourself toward the group and keep your head up
- Do not speak into your notes
- Avoid shouting over others as this may cause strain
- Use eye contact to indicate that you wish to make a contribution. Identify who is chairing the meeting and establish eye contact with that person. A good chairperson should be looking for such non-verbal cues
- If possible, sit where the person leading or chairing the meeting can see you. It will prove much easier for that person to pick up gestures and eye contact, indicating you wish to speak

PRACTICE READING

Exercise 26

This reading will allow you to practise some of the techniques we have covered in this pocketbook. Repeat it each week, concentrating on a different aspect of vocal skills each time – eg clarity, pace, sustaining the energy throughout each phrase.

Reading

With my stepping ashore I began the most unhappy part of my adventures. It was half-past twelve in the morning, and though the wind was broken by land, it was a cold night. I dared not sit down, for I thought I should have frozen, but took off my shoes and walked to and fro upon the sand, barefoot, and beating my breast with infinite weariness. There was no sound of man or cattle, not a cock crew, although it was about the hour of their first waking. Only the surf broke outside in the distance, which put me in mind of my perils and those of my friend. To walk by the sea at that hour of the morning, and in a place so desert-like and lonesome, struck me with a kind of fear.

136 words

OTHER KEY CONSIDERATIONS

ASSESSMENT SHEET –
A USEFUL RESOURCE

Presenter/Teacher's Name: _____

Observer: _____

Date: _____ Time: _____ Venue: _____

Orientation: Good (always faced the audience when speaking) ❑
Adequate (faced the audience when speaking most of the time) ❑
Needs improvement (did not face the audience when speaking) ❑

Posture: Good (posture was upright and the body was in alignment) ❑
Adequate (posture was generally appropriate most of the time) ❑
Needs improvement (posture was poor) ❑

Yes/No

Was there obvious tension present in any area of the body?
If so, please detail in which area of the body the tension was apparent.

Continued...

Did the presenter/teacher start their first phrase on a full breath?	Yes/No
Did the teacher/presenter stop for breath at appropriate points?	Yes/No/Sometimes
Did the presenter/teacher run out of breath at any point?	Yes/No

Rate the presenter/teacher for:

Audibility:	Good/Adequate/Poor
Clarity:	Good/Adequate/Poor
Vitality:	Good/Adequate/Poor
Pacing:	Good/Adequate/Poor

Did the teacher/presenter pause frequently?	Yes/No
Was the energy sustained throughout each phrase?	Yes/No/Most of the time
Were there pitch glides at appropriate points during the speech?	Yes/No/Sometimes
Did the presenter/teacher use emphasis to energise the delivery?	Yes/No/Sometimes
Were there variances in volume?	Yes/No/Sometimes

Other comments:

OTHER KEY CONSIDERATIONS

AFTERTHOUGHT

You may be a little overwhelmed at the thought of trying to put into practice, when presenting or teaching, everything covered in this pocketbook. You may feel that you have enough of a challenge merely thinking of what to say or do next, without the added challenge of thinking about the actual sound you are making.

Don't feel that you have to achieve everything at once. Instead concentrate on one aspect of your voice at a time and work on that.

A goal is much easier to achieve if it is broken down into manageable chunks.

About the Author

Richard Payne MA, FITOL, Cert. Ed., Chartered MCIPD.
Richard is an experienced and popular voice tutor who has
worked with: individuals, teachers, lecturers, professionals and
business people. He is also Managing Director of BSPS Training
Consultancy Limited and a regular contributor of articles to
various journals and publications. Richard is a Member of Equity,
and The Institute of Training and Occupational Learning.
He is also a Chartered Member of The Chartered Institute of
Personnel and Development. Richard's combination of pragmatic
advice and accelerated learning techniques has helped thousands
of people to make the most of their voice when presenting or teaching.

Contact
Richard Payne,
Managing Director, BSPS Training Consultancy, PO Box 10549,
Sutton Coldfield, West Midlands, B72 1ZH

Tel: +44 (0) 121 355 4320
website: www.bspstraining.co.uk   e-mail: richardpayne@bspstraining.co.uk

THE MANAGEMENT POCKETBOOK SERIES

Pocketbooks (also available in e-book format)

360 Degree Feedback	Flexible Workplace	Meetings	Succeeding at Interviews
Absence Management	Handling Complaints	Mentoring	Talent Management
Appraisals	Icebreakers	Motivation	Teambuilding Activities
Assertiveness	Impact & Presence	Negotiator's	Teamworking
Balance Sheet	Improving Efficiency	Networking	Telephone Skills
Business Planning	Improving Profitability	NLP	Telesales
Business Writing	Induction	Nurturing Innovation	Thinker's
Call Centre Customer Care	Influencing	Openers & Closers	Time Management
Career Transition	International Trade	People Manager's	Trainer Standards
Coaching	Interviewer's	Performance Management	Trainer's
Communicator's	I.T. Trainer's	Personal Success	Training Evaluation
Competencies	Key Account Manager's	Positive Mental Attitude	Training Needs Analysis
Creative Manager's	Leadership	Presentations	Virtual Teams
C.R.M.	Learner's	Problem Behaviour	Vocal Skills
Cross-cultural Business	Management Models	Problem Solving	Working Relationships
Customer Service	Manager's	Project Management	Workplace Politics
Decision-making	Managing Budgets	Psychometric Testing	
Delegation	Managing Cashflow	Resolving Conflict	
Developing People	Managing Change	Reward	**Pocketfiles**
Diversity	Managing Customer Service	Sales Excellence	
Emotional Intelligence	Managing Difficult Participants	Salesperson's	Trainer's Blue Pocketfile of
Employment Law	Managing Recruitment	Self-managed Development	Ready-to-use Activities
Empowerment	Managing Upwards	Starting In Management	
Energy and Well-being	Managing Your Appraisal	Strategy	Trainer's Green Pocketfile of
Facilitator's	Marketing	Stress	Ready-to-use Activities
			Trainer's Red Pocketfile of
			Ready-to-use Activities

22.05.09

Your details

Name _____

Position _____

Company _____

Address _____

_____

_____

Telephone _____

Fax _____

E-mail _____

VAT No. (EC companies) _____

Your Order Ref _____

Please send me:

		No. copies
The Vocal Skills	Pocketbook	
The _____	Pocketbook	
The _____	Pocketbook	
The _____	Pocketbook	

Order by Post
MANAGEMENT
POCKETBOOKS LTD
LAUREL HOUSE, STATION APPROACH,
ALRESFORD, HAMPSHIRE SO24 9JH UK

Order by Phone, Fax or Internet
Telephone: +44 (0)1962 735573
Facsimile: +44 (0)1962 733637
E-mail: sales@pocketbook.co.uk
Web: www.pocketbook.co.uk

Customers in USA should contact:
Management Pocketbooks
2427 Bond Street, University Park, IL 60466
Telephone: 866 620 6944 Facsimile: 708 534 7803
E-mail: mp.orders@ware-pak.com
Web: www.managementpocketbooks.com

Answers to Exercise 20 (page 77):

F Top teeth on the lower lip. Air escapes to make an audible friction. There is no voice when this sound is produced.

V As above but there is a voice when this sound is produced.

B Complete closure of the lips with air pressure building up behind them which is released suddenly. This sound is produced with a voice.

P As above but with no voice.

T The tongue tip comes into contact with the place where the upper teeth meet the hard palate. No voice.

D As above but with a voice.

Th The tongue is placed between the teeth. Air escapes through the gap in the teeth. There sound is produced with a voice.

Th As above but without a voice.

M The lips are brought together and air escapes down the nose. This sound is produced with a voice.

N The tongue tip comes into contact with the place where the upper teeth meet the hard palate. Air is released through the nose. This sound is produced with a voice.

Acknowledgement

The readings on pages 82 and 105 have been taken from, respectively, *Tale of Two Cities* by Charles Dickens and *Robinson Crusoe* by Daniel Defoe. All other readings are either of the author's creation or are taken from sources that both author and publisher have tried, unsuccessfully, to locate. The origin of Exercise 19 on page 72 we have been unable to identify as well.